群鷺

First published 2022
© Tung Ken Lam 2022

Published by Wooden Books Ltd.
Glastonbury, Somerset
www.woodenbooks.com

British Library Cataloguing in Publication Data
Lam, T.K.
Origami

A CIP catalogue record for this book
may be obtained from the British Library

ISBN-10: 1-907155-45-7
ISBN-13: 978-1-907155-45-1

Designed and typeset in Glastonbury, UK.

Printed in China on FSC® certified papers by
RR Donnelley Asia Printing Solutions Ltd.

ORIGAMI

FROM SURFACE TO FORM

Tung Ken Lam

I am indebted to the many paperfolders of the past and present from whose ideas and research much of this book has been distilled, including: Margherita Piazzola Beloch, David Collier, Erik and Martin Demaine, Amy C. Edmonson, Peter Engel, Martin Gardner, Michel Grand, Kazuo Haga, Hatori Koshiro, Tom Hull, Dard Hunter, Paul Jackson, Jun Maekawa, Jacques Justin, Kunihiko Kasahara, Fumiaki Kawahata, Toshikazu Kawasaki, Eric Kenneway, Richard Duks Koschitz, Robert Lang, Toshiyuki Meguro, Sue Pope, Jean & Samuel Randlett, Joseph O'Rourke, Akira Yoshizawa and the unknown folders known as Traditional. Special thanks to Matt Tweed and John Martineau for their superlative editing and design work.

Work is credited to the creators where known; p. vi: after Origami Profiles by John Smith; 14: Butterfly, after Akira Yoshizawa; 20 & 21: Koi & Jumping Frog, Nippon Origami Association; 22: Dog Base, John Montroll; 23: Elephant, George Rhoads; 32: Approximate Regular Pentagon, David Collier; Cairo Tiling, David Mitchell; 37: Skeletal Octahedron, Robert Neale; 43: Trihexaflexagon, Arthur Stone; 46: Waterbomb & Chevron Corrugations, Shuzo Fujimoto & others; 48: Yoshimura Shelter, Yoshimaru Yoshimura; 49: Miura-Ori, Koryo Miura; Deployable Structure, after Sergio Pellegrino & others; 50: Skeletal Icosidodecahedron, R. Buckminster Fuller; 53: Hexagonal Tower & Arches, David Huffman; Mushroom, Vincent Floderer. All others are traditional except those by the author; p. 13: Hand; 15: Three-piece Tiger, after David Mitchell; 33: Islamic Design & Parquet Deformation; 36: Pentagram, 37: Six- & Four-pointed Stars; 38: Windowed Icosahedron; 39: Double Equilateral Unit; 40: Skeletal Cuboctahedron; 41: WXYZ & XYZ Rhombic; 43: Woven Cube; 55: Unicorn. More at www.foldworks.net.

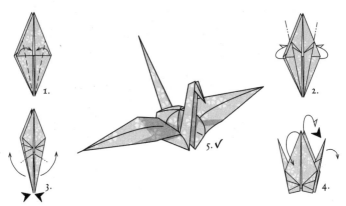

ABOVE and FRONTISPIECE: the ORIZURU 鶴 or CRANE is probably the most famous Japanese origami design and has become a symbol of peace. 1. Start with a bird base (page 19, step 10), fold sides to centre. 2. Repeat for reverse. 3. Crease and reverse fold neck and tail. 4. Reverse fold head. 5. Open out and spread wings. Traditionally, folding a thousand cranes is said to grant a wish.

CONTENTS

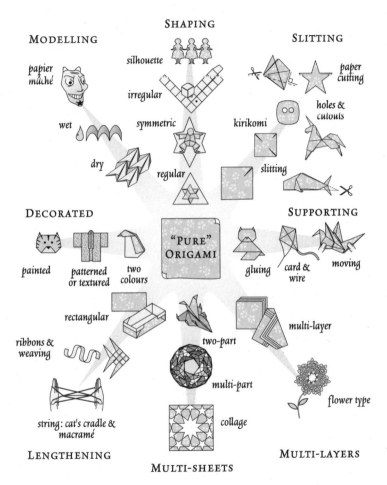

SHAPING

MODELLING

SLITTING

papier mâché

silhouette

paper cutting

irregular

holes & cutouts

wet

symmetric

kirikomi

dry

regular

slitting

DECORATED

"PURE" ORIGAMI

SUPPORTING

painted

patterned or textured

two colours

gluing

card & wire

moving

rectangular

multi-layer

ribbons & weaving

two-part

multi-part

flower type

string: cat's cradle & macramé

collage

LENGTHENING

MULTI-LAYERS

MULTI-SHEETS

Relaxing the "purity" of origami leads to different kinds of crafts. The "closed-system" nature of origami is characterised by its ability to create a model and yet return to the starting point. After John Smith [1924–2018].

INTRODUCTION

We have all folded paper in our lives. Folding a letter to fit an envelope, or simply closing a book: these are everyday examples. More playful are the paper boats, hats and airplanes of childhood.

A diploma is a certificate for successful study. The word derives from the Greek *diplōma* "folded paper"—*diploun* 'to fold' and *diplous* 'double'. Curiously, the Japanese word "*origami*" also means a certificate: it is a sheet of paper folded in half to attest the provenance of a work of art.

Even the simplest folded paper can yield remarkable mathematics. In the last few decades, the mathematics of origami has grown to be an important field of research, spanning design, engineering, geometry and number theory. For example, origami can solve cubic equations that cannot be solved with a straight edge and a pair of compasses.

The complexity and sophistication of origami design has also increased in recent times. For some, folding one paper square without cuts has spurred innovations, like insects with clearly defined appendages or animals with all their toes individually folded. Another approach combines modules folded from multiple sheets to create polyhedra and other geometrical shapes. A third technique pleats, twists and corrugates single sheets into remarkable forms. These approaches may use conventional straight folds, or employ curved folds to produce an even greater variety of outcomes.

Origami is a practical and enjoyable way to learn mathematics and science, so be sure to have a good supply of paper squares and rectangles to try out the ideas in this book. 80 gsm A4 printer paper and memo cube paper are both convenient sources.

FOLDING PAPER
greet the sheet

There can be no paperfolding without paper. The great sinologist Joseph Needham [1900–95] wrote that "of all the products from the ancient world, few can compare in significance with the Chinese inventions of paper and printing." Paper was used for clothing, armour, sanitation and packaging as well as writing, printing and money.

折紙, "fold paper" in Chinese, is pronounced *oru* (fold) *kami* (paper) in Japanese. *Origami* has since become the dominant term in English.

The best paper for folding is strong and holds a crease. Thin paper (with a weight of 40-60 gsm) is better for origami, whilst thicker paper (80-120 gsm) can be used for larger models. Some household papers can be used, although newspaper is weak and doesn't crease well.

Commercial *kami* origami paper frequently comes in 15 cm (6 inch) squares. Typically 60 gsm, it is white on one side, coloured or patterned on the other, and is convenient and pleasant to use.

Strong and light, with a soft, fabric-like texture, *washi* is a translucent Japanese paper, often handmade from the bark of the paper mulberry tree. A Korean paper, *hanji*, shares many of its characteristics. *Chiyogami* is a strong, colourfully printed washi paper that will not rip. Its strength is due to the long fibres used in the pulp: most machine-made papers have short fibres which make them weak by comparison.

LEFT: Papermaking in the 17th century: the vatman, coucher and layman at work. Typically, paper is made from wood or cotton fibres pounded with water into a pulp. This is spread onto a screen, then dried and pressed into a thin flexible sheet.

FACING: The wasp is possibly the world's first papermaker. The queen starts her nest by chewing wood and plant fibres together with saliva to make a grey papery material.

BELOW: Fancy napkin folding: An illustrated page from Li tre trattati di messer Mattia Giegher Bavaro di Mosburc, Matthias Giegher, Padua, 1629.

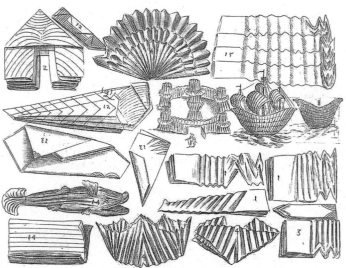

FOLDS & SYMBOLS
the language of origami

Printed and illustrated instructions for folding paper are relatively recent. Traditionally, the art of paperfolding was learned in person.

Modern origami instructions distinguish the two main folds using different types of lines and arrows. The basic **VALLEY FOLD** is a concave fold in the paper. When turned over, the valley becomes a convex **MOUNTAIN FOLD** (*right*).

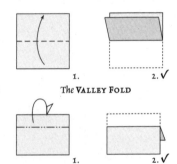

The **VALLEY FOLD**

The **MOUNTAIN FOLD**

Make sharp accurate folds on a table or clean flat surface. Pick up the lower corner or edge and sweep up to align with the top. Keep the paper in place with one hand and use the other to press it flat: carefully smooth down and then flatten to the left and right (*below*).

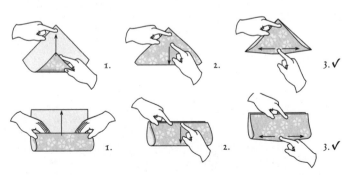

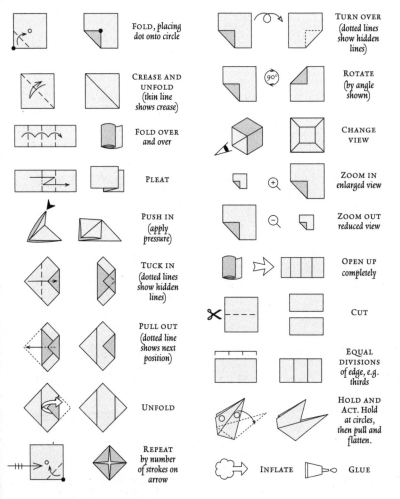

FOLD, *placing dot onto circle*	**TURN OVER** *(dotted lines show hidden lines)*
CREASE AND UNFOLD *(thin line shows crease)*	**ROTATE** *(by angle shown)*
FOLD OVER *and over*	**CHANGE VIEW**
PLEAT	**ZOOM IN** *enlarged view*
PUSH IN *(apply pressure)*	**ZOOM OUT** *reduced view*
TUCK IN *(dotted lines show hidden lines)*	**OPEN UP** *completely*
PULL OUT *(dotted line shows next position)*	**CUT**
UNFOLD	**EQUAL DIVISIONS** *of edge, e.g. thirds*
REPEAT *by number of strokes on arrow*	**HOLD AND ACT.** *Hold at circles, then pull and flatten.*
	INFLATE **GLUE**

ABOVE: basic **FOLDS** and **SYMBOLS**. *Dotted lines show the next position or reveal hidden lines.*

5

STARTING SHAPES
special rectangles

Much traditional origami is made from a single square, a shape which has cultural and spiritual significance all around the world. Squares are the same everywhere, while the proportions of other rectangular sheets of paper can vary enormously. Some common rectangles are shown here, along with folding instructions and examples. Some are used in this book, others (like the golden rectangle) are rare in origami.

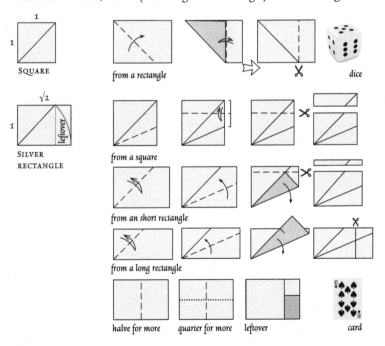

SQUARE

from a rectangle

dice

SILVER RECTANGLE

from a square

from an short rectangle

from a long rectangle

halve for more   quarter for more   leftover   card

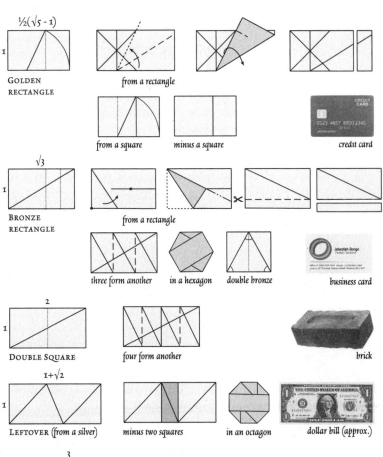

$\frac{1}{2}(\sqrt{5}-1)$

1

GOLDEN RECTANGLE

from a rectangle

from a square   *minus a square*   *credit card*

$\sqrt{3}$

1

BRONZE RECTANGLE

from a rectangle

three form another   *in a hexagon*   *double bronze*   *business card*

2

1

DOUBLE SQUARE

four form another   *brick*

$1+\sqrt{2}$

1

LEFTOVER *(from a silver)*

minus two squares   *in an octagon*   *dollar bill (approx.)*

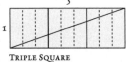

3

1

TRIPLE SQUARE

ABOVE & FACING: *Although the* **SQUARE** *is the primary starting point for much origami, a few other* **RECTANGLES** *are shown here, some of which we will meet later in this book.*

7

PAPER HATS
if you want to get ahead

An early use of paper was for clothing. Paper lining improved heat insulation and paper armour even provided protection in battle.

Making hats has long been a tradition. The **NEWSPAPER HAT** turns into a floating **PAPER BOAT,** and is the starting point for the practical **POINTED HAT** and **PRINTER'S CAP**. Both have many layers at the front to absorb the wearers' perspiration as they work (*below and opposite*).

  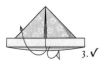

The **NEWSPAPER HAT**. 1. *Start with a rectangle folded in half, short edges together. Fold the corners.* 2. *Fold up the bottom edge and fold up again. Repeat behind.* 3. *Open out and wear.*

The **PAPER BOAT**. *Start with the The Newspaper Hat*. 1. *Fold the tip up. Repeat behind.* 2. *Open up and flatten.* 3. *Pull the tips up and away. At the same time, let the front and rear bottom edges move up.* 4. *Shape these folds to finish the boat.*

The **POINTED HAT**. 1. *Start at step 2 of the Newspaper Hat, folding up rear edge.* 2. *Fold up the bottom edge and then fold over again.* 3. *Open out.*

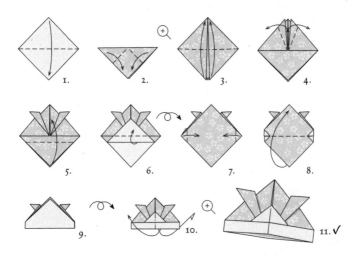

The **KABUTO** 兜. This Japanese samurai helmet is a traditional fold. The final circumference is about half the paper length, so a square of newspaper should fit the head. The first two steps are easier if turned through 180° then the bottom corner can be folded up to the top. Make a corner bookmark from a 75 mm square by finishing at step 6 and tucking in the rear flap.

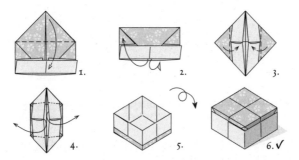

The **PRINTER'S CAP**. 1. Start with the Pointed Hat. Fold top point down and tuck behind the bottom uppermost flap. 2. Open up for a basic cap, or for the printer's cap: 3. Open and flatten. Fold and tuck sides into the middle. 4. Open out. 5. Straighten sides, then 6. flip over.

WRAPS, CUPS & BOXES
pots for pills, powders & potions

Paper has long been used to wrap goods and protect fragile items. The **MAGAZINE BOX** can be folded from pages taken from a magazine. Use it as a wastebasket or a container for small items (*opposite top*). Make a second box with the same sized paper to fit as a lid.

You can drink from the **PAPER CUP** if you use a clean sheet of paper. This design was taught to soldiers in the field so that they could skim scum from the surface of water. The cup can be worn as a hat if made with a large enough square of paper (*opposite, lower*).

In the past, letters were not sent in envelopes, they were folded and sealed with a drop of wax. You can fold your own **ENVELOPE** (*below, upper*). This is best for hand delivery as postal services disapprove of open edges trapping other mail. The **WRAP** (*below, lower*) makes a quick yet practical container for medicinal powders.

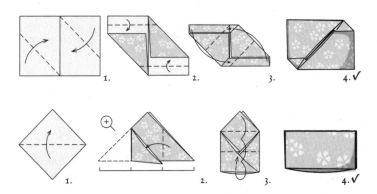

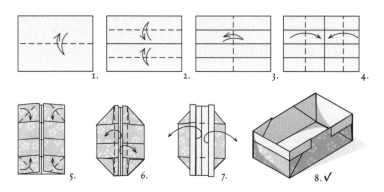

The **MAGAZINE BOX**. 1. Use A4 or A5. Fold long edges together and unfold. 2. Fold long edges into centre and unfold. 3. Fold short sides to centre. 4. Fold short sides together and unfold. 5. Fold corners onto quarter lines. 6. Fold raw edges out from the centre over the folded corners. 7. Open out. 8. Finished box. Fold a second from the same sized paper to make a lid.

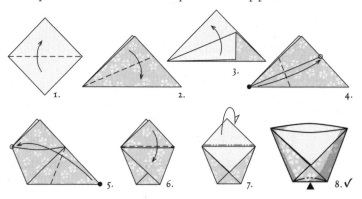

The **PAPER CUP**. 1. Fold a diagonal of a square. 2. Bisect the 45° angle on left hand side: fold the short left edge onto the longest edge. 3. Unfold. 4. Fold left corner over onto the end of crease line. 5. Fold the right corner on to left corner. 6. Valley top flap down over edge. 7. Mountain fold the top flap behind. 8. Open the cup out and pinch the bottom.

11

PRELIMINARY FOLDS
& waterbomb basics

Squares naturally fold in half lengthwise or diagonally. The most accurate method is to fold and then unfold each 'mirror line'.

For a **PRELIMINARY FOLD**, start with the diagonals, then turn over for the short mirror lines (*below 1-4*). Although less precise, the alternative method (*below i-iv*) shows *igai-sei*—an element of surprise.

The **WATERBOMB BASE** has four flaps, making it a versatile foundation for many models. Begin with the short mirror lines then turn over to fold the diagonals (*opposite top*). Although the centre of the square is not a free flap, it forms the thumb of the **HAND** (*lower, opposite*).

The two bases share the same folds and are essentially each other's inverse: push in the centre to transform one into the other.

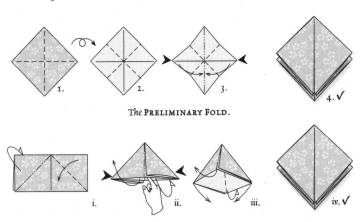

The **PRELIMINARY FOLD**.

An alternative method of creating a **PRELIMINARY FOLD**.

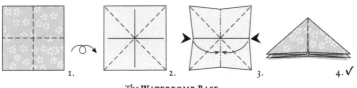

The **WATERBOMB BASE**.

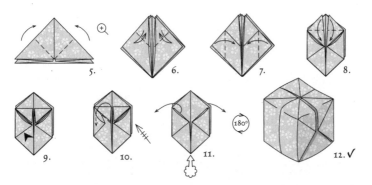

To complete the **WATERBOMB**: continue with steps 5-9 then, 10. Tuck in flaps, repeat for all four sides. 11. Blow into the hole at the base to inflate. Fill with water to devastating effect!

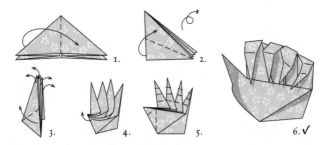

The **HAND**. 1. Start with a waterbomb base. 2. Fold all flaps to the right. 3. Fold all layers (the original edges of the square) onto the hypotenuse. Turn over. 4. Spread the fingertips, and the thumb will rise. 5. Press flat. 6. Bend the fingers and make the thumb.

EASY ORIGAMI
a little animal magic

Nature inspires many origami models. Both the elegant **SWAN** and the **PAPER TIGER** can be folded by small hands (*opposite*). Make the tiger super ferocious by using orange squares and giving it stripes.

Begin the **BUTTERFLY** (*below, upper*) with a waterbomb base (*page 13*). Another waterbomb base, this time at the top of an oblong, starts the **HOPPING FROG**. To make the frog hop, press down on its back, then slip finger off. For more spring, add paper into the legs. (*below, lower*).

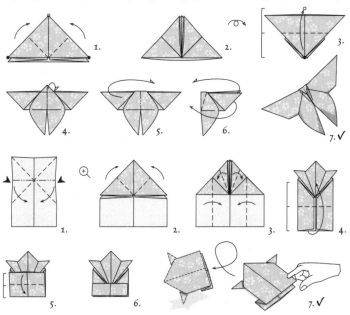

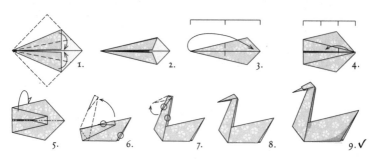

The **SWAN**. Note how the reverse folds are made in a simple way.

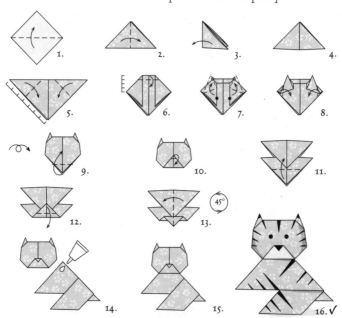

The **PAPER TIGER** is made of three squares: one for the head (1–10) and two for the body (11–13).
The first two folds are the same for each part. Glue head onto body and decorate.

15

MORE COMPLEX FOLDS
petals, squashes, rabbits & reverses

The folds on these pages involve making more than one fold at a time. All use the black chevron symbol ➤, which means 'apply pressure'.

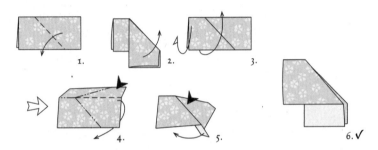

The **INSIDE REVERSE FOLD**. Open the paper and push in the right side. Change the mountain folds to the right and front into valley folds. Flatten.

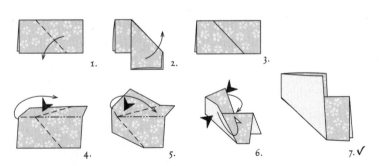

The **OUTSIDE REVERSE FOLD**. Open the paper and push the point from which the creases radiate. Change the mountain folds to the left and rear into valley folds. Flatten.

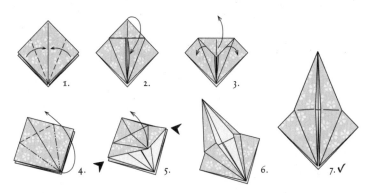

The **PETAL FOLD**. Begin with a preliminary fold (page 12). Hold the single layer of paper at bottom and lift flap upwards. Simultaneously pull the sides towards the middle and flatten.

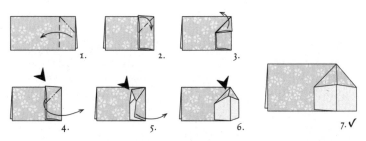

The **SQUASH**. Use a finger to open the pocket. Slide finger upwards to fully open pocket, then use the other hand to flatten.

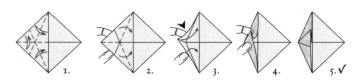

The **RABBIT EAR FOLD**. Precrease two angle bisectors and one perpendicular bisector. Pinch together the two long edges to form a flap. Raise this flap and flatten to one side.

BIRDS & PLANES
paperfolding in action

The best origami is not only enjoyable to make but also has an added feature to enhance the experience.

The **FLAPPING BIRD** (*opposite top*) was brought to Europe by Japanese performers who appeared to make squares of paper transform instantly into birds. The secret was to precrease the squares: the creases were hidden by the bright stage lights. Note that the **BIRD BASE** (*steps 1-10*) creates a flexible starting point for many other models.

Beloved in classrooms everywhere, the **PAPER PLANE** is a childhood classic (*opposite, lower*). Modern plane designs can fly for up to 30 seconds depending on the rules followed, *e.g.* using a single sheet only, adding weights like paperclips, or cutting and taping.

Pleasing and elegant, the **DOCKING SPACESHIPS** (*below*) deftly combine two standard bases—a waterbomb base (*page 13*) for the **INTERCEPTOR** (*steps 1-3*), and a petal fold (*page 17*) for the **MOTHERSHIP** (*steps a-c*). Its provenance is uncertain, though it may be from 1970s Hong Kong.

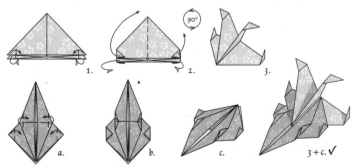

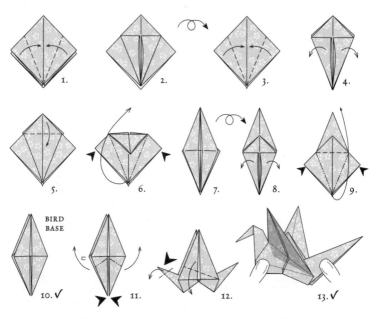

ABOVE: The traditional **FLAPPING BIRD**. 1. Start with a preliminary fold (page 12). 2-9. Petal fold (page 17): hold the bottom and lift flap. Pull sides towards middle and flatten. Repeat for reverse. 10. Completed **BIRD BASE**. 11. Inside reverse fold neck and tail, starting folds a bit below centre. 12. Reverse fold head. Curl or fold wings. 13. Hold chest and pull to flap the wings. BELOW: the ubiquitous **PAPER PLANE**. Try folding small flaps on the wings to create ailerons, allowing your flying machine to turn. Add a paperclip to the nose for greater stability.

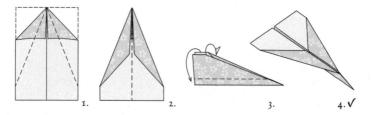

FISH & FROGS
underwater wonders

These aquatic models introduce another pair of standard origami bases. As usual, sharp, accurate folds get the best results.

The **KOI** 鯉 (*below*) uses a **FISH BASE** (*steps 1-4*) as its foundation. In Japan, koi are customarily folded on Children's Day in May. Several can be attached to poles to make *koi-nobori*, carp streamers.

The more difficult **JUMPING FROG** (*opposite*) uses the **FROG BASE** (*steps 1-12*) which needs both petal and reverse folds. To make the frog jump, stroke its back with a finger and let it slip off.

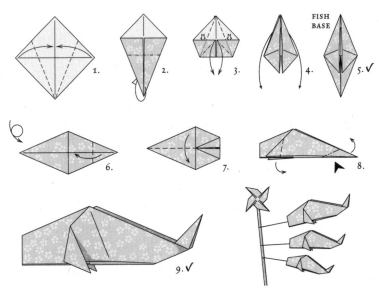

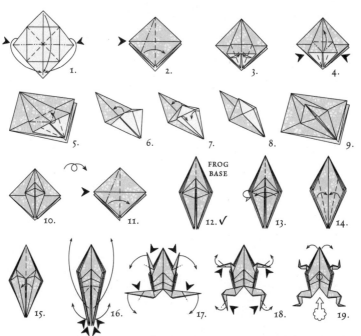

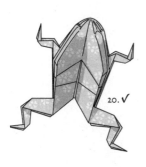

The **JUMPING FROG**. 1. Use a 15 cm square. Start with a preliminary fold (page 12). 2. Take one flap and flatten symmetrically. 3. Precrease. 4-8. Petal fold (page 17): lift flap and fold upwards. Open pocket and collapse sides of flaps towards middle. 9. Petal fold complete. 10. Turn over. 11. Repeat for the other three flaps. 12. **FROG BASE** complete. 13. Fold a single right flap to left. Turn over and repeat. This exposes faces without triangular flaps. 14. Narrow flaps. Leave a small gap in the middle so that flaps are not crushed when folding whole flap in the next step. 15. Repeat for other faces. 16. Make legs with inside reverse folds. 17. Reverse fold knees. 18. Reverse fold feet. 19. Blow into hole at base to inflate. 20. Completed frog.

CREASE PATTERNS
the key to analysis and design

Unfolding a piece of origami reveals its structural *crease pattern*. Crease patterns provide a way to analyse the classic bases—for instance, the bird base combines four kite folds, and a frog base is four fish bases.

Another way to consider origami is to focus on the *flaps*—those parts of a model which move freely without affecting the rest. Designs are predicated by the number, length and connection of flaps. For example, the **CRANE** requires five: two for the head and tail, two for the wings and one stubby flap for the back. *Blintz* versions of the bases cunningly add extra flaps by diagonally folding the corners to the centre, and then folding the classic base from the resulting square.

Classic bases develop two or four flaps at the corners of the initial square, plus an occasional small central one. Their arrangement can be seen as full or partial circles, optimally packed inside a square (*opposite*).

Moving beyond the classic bases has allowed for design innovations, such as John Montroll's six flap **DOG BASE** (*below*). The large head is easily folded into details like ears, jaws and eyes. Note that two corners have been sacrificed to make the paper into an irregular hexagon.

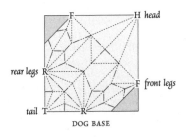

DOG BASE

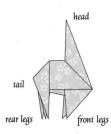

22

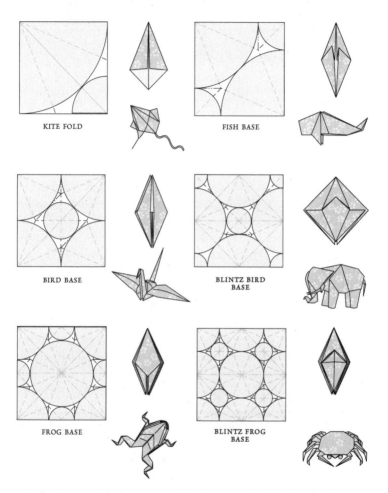

KITE FOLD

FISH BASE

BIRD BASE

BLINTZ BIRD BASE

FROG BASE

BLINTZ FROG BASE

The **CLASSIC ORIGAMI BASES** are named after the most popular subjects into which they are folded. Here the circles emphasize the distribution of the flaps within the crease patterns.

23

FLAT VERTEX THEOREMS
& the problem of halving

When analysing crease patterns, the interactions of all the folds have to be considered. The number of folds meeting at a vertex constitutes its *degree*, e.g. four folds join at a *degree-4 vertex*. Vertices that can be completely flattened must have an even degree, as odd degrees can never fold flat. In general, even if individual vertices can be folded flat, it does not necessarily follow that the entire pattern will also do so.

Independently described by Jun Maekawa and Jacques Justin in the 1980s, the **MAEKAWA-JUSTIN THEOREM** predicted that the difference between the number of mountain and valley folds will always be two. Another theorem, the **KAWASAKI-JUSTIN**, observed by Justin and Toshikazu Kawasaki, states that at a vertex that folds flat, the alternating (i.e. added then subtracted) sum of consecutive angles equals zero, and thus complementary angles will add to 180° (*opposite, top*).

It was long believed that repeatedly **HALVING** a piece of paper more than seven times was impossible, as each fold exponentially increases the thickness whilst simultaneously reducing the available length. However in 2002, student Britney Gallivan managed to fold a 4000 foot piece of thin tissue in half twelve times—the first person to achieve more than nine. Her key insight was to model the way paper is "lost" with each halving (*opposite, lower*).

If it were possible to fold a sheet of 80 gsm A4 in half 50 times, the thickness would be about 10^{11} m, or two thirds of the average distance between the sun and earth. Conversely, the length of the folded paper would shrink to 3×10^{-16} m, which is several orders of magnitude smaller than the radius of a hydrogen atom.

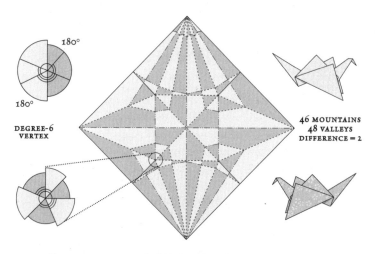

180°

180°

DEGREE-6 VERTEX

46 MOUNTAINS
48 VALLEYS
DIFFERENCE = 2

FLAT VERTEX THEORY: For a flat folding model, the crease pattern can be filled with two colours so that no adjacent polygons are the same. Refolded, one side will be one colour, the other side the second. Vertices are all even degree, with the sum of alternate angles being 180°. The difference between the number of mountain (M) and valley folds (V) is always two: |M-V|=2.

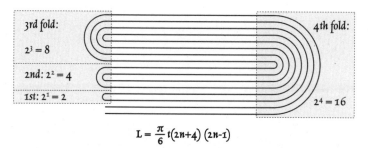

3rd fold:

$2^3 = 8$

2nd: $2^2 = 4$

1st: $2^1 = 2$

4th fold:

$2^4 = 16$

$$L = \frac{\pi}{6} t(2n+4)(2n-1)$$

GALLIVAN'S FORMULA gives the length lost to the fold when a piece of paper is halved, (L, shaded section), where t is the paper thickness and n is the number of folds. The number of layers rapidly grows exponentially: shown here is the situation after only four folds.

THE AXIOMS OF ORIGAMI
the seven fold way

Classical geometry studied constructions using an unmarked straight edge and a pair of compasses, and was able to solve *quadratic* equations. By contrast, origami may be applied to solve *cubic* equations: this was found by Margherita Piazzola Beloch [1879–1976] in the mid-1930s, when she applied paperfolding to Eduard Lill's [1830–1900] graphical method of solving of equations of the third degree.

Seven different kinds of folds are possible: these are known as the **ORIGAMI AXIOMS** (*below and opposite*). Note that some axioms need translucent paper or a strong light to make lines and points visible.

Consider the sixth axiom: this puts one point on a line and a second point onto another line. The ability to do two things simultaneously gives origami more power than straight edge and compasses constructions, making it possible to determine $^3\sqrt{2}$ or trisect angles (*see page 31*).

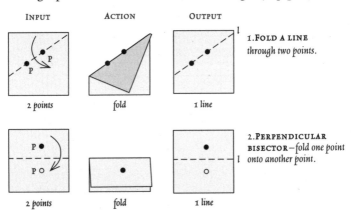

INPUT   ACTION   OUTPUT

1. **FOLD A LINE**
through two points.

2 points   fold   1 line

2. **PERPENDICULAR BISECTOR** – *fold one point onto another point.*

2 points   fold   1 line

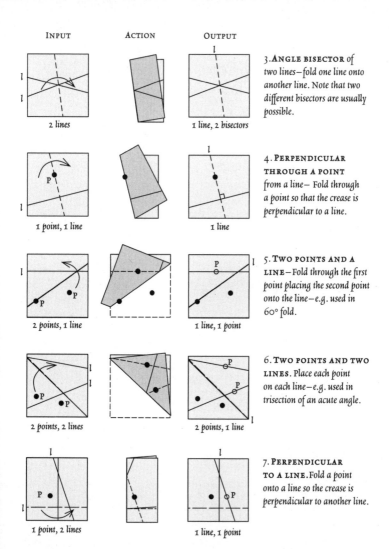

INPUT	ACTION	OUTPUT	

3. ANGLE BISECTOR of two lines—fold one line onto another line. Note that two different bisectors are usually possible.

2 lines → 1 line, 2 bisectors

4. PERPENDICULAR THROUGH A POINT from a line— Fold through a point so that the crease is perpendicular to a line.

1 point, 1 line → 1 line

5. TWO POINTS AND A LINE—Fold through the first point placing the second point onto the line—e.g. used in 60° fold.

2 points, 1 line → 1 line, 1 point

6. TWO POINTS AND TWO LINES. Place each point on each line—e.g. used in trisection of an acute angle.

2 points, 2 lines → 2 points, 1 line

7. PERPENDICULAR TO A LINE. Fold a point onto a line so the crease is perpendicular to another line.

1 point, 2 lines → 1 line, 1 point

27

HARMONY IN A SQUARE
Haga's theorems & more

A square's edge is easily divided into halves, quarters, and eighths, etc, but *odd* divisions like thirds and fifths are harder. Five ways to divide an edge into thirds are shown (*below*). Curling the paper (*a*) is simple, accurate and leaves the fewest creases. Using a reference sheet of parallel lines (*b*) is an ancient way of creating any fraction along any edge. Tomako Fuse's technique folds a corner on to a centre-line (*c*), while Masamichi Noma's solution folds two quarter marks together to produce the third (*d*). Most of these techniques can be applied to other fractions too (*e.g. see the list of examples for the diagonal line technique, e*).

The three connected theorems of Professor Kazuo Haga [1934–] (*shown opposite*) elegantly constructs one third and other fractions.

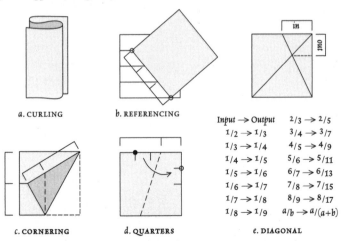

a. CURLING   b. REFERENCING

c. CORNERING   d. QUARTERS   e. DIAGONAL

Input $\to$ Output		
$1/2 \to 1/3$	$2/3 \to 2/5$	
$1/3 \to 1/4$	$3/4 \to 3/7$	
$1/4 \to 1/5$	$4/5 \to 4/9$	
$1/5 \to 1/6$	$5/6 \to 5/11$	
$1/6 \to 1/7$	$6/7 \to 6/13$	
$1/7 \to 1/8$	$7/8 \to 7/15$	
$1/8 \to 1/9$	$8/9 \to 8/17$	
	$a/b \to a/(a+b)$	

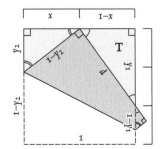

x	y_1	$1-y_1$	$1-x$	d	y_2	y_2
	$\dfrac{2x}{1+x}$	$\dfrac{1-x}{1+x}$	$1-x$	$\dfrac{1+x^2}{1+x}$	$\dfrac{1-x^2}{2}$	$\dfrac{1+x^2}{2}$
$1/2 \rightarrow$	$2/3$	$1/3$	$1/2$	$5/6$	$3/8$	$5/8$
$1/3 \rightarrow$	$1/2$	$1/2$	$2/3$	$5/6$	$4/9$	$5/9$
$2/3 \rightarrow$	$4/5$	$1/5$	$1/3$	$13/15$	$5/18$	$13/18$
$3/4 \rightarrow$	$6/7$	$1/7$	$1/4$	$25/28$	$7/32$	$25/32$

ABOVE: **HAGA'S 1ST THEOREM** uses Pythagoras' theorem to create fractions from other fractions. If x is a rational fraction, then all the other lengths marked on the square above will be rational fractions too. The illustration shows x as one half, and outputs thirds on the right.

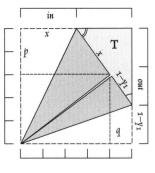

LEFT: **HAGA'S 2ND THEOREM**. This example converts $1/2$ (at the top), into $2/3$ (down the right side). Amazingly, the point where the two flaps meet also determines $1/5$ (q, along the bottom edge) and $2/5$ (p, along the left edge), shown in dotted lines. Furthermore, the two flaps also have short edges of length $1/2$ and $1/3$, to give a total length of $5/6$. RIGHT: Another construction for $1/5$ and $2/5$ using midpoints.

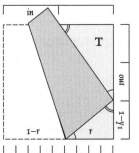

LEFT: **HAGA'S 3RD THEOREM**. All three of Haga's theorems achieve the same triangle T. The 3rd theorem creates a measure r, along the bottom edge, which divides the bottom edge into $4/9$ and $5/9$ when the input is $1/2$ as shown.

x	p	q	r
	$\dfrac{2x^2}{1+x^2}$	$\dfrac{(x-1)^2}{x^2+1}$	$\dfrac{2x}{(1+x)^2}$
$1/2 \rightarrow$	$2/5$	$1/5$	$4/9$
$1/3 \rightarrow$	$1/5$	$2/5$	$3/8$
$2/3 \rightarrow$	$8/13$	$1/13$	$12/25$
$3/4 \rightarrow$	$18/25$	$1/25$	$24/49$

DIVIDING ANGLES
halves, thirds & fifths

One simple fold can divide an angle (*axiom 3, page 27*). Fold again and you can quarter it or divide it into eighths (*opposite, top left*). But how would you *trisect* an angle (i.e. divide it into three)? It is impossible to trisect all but the most basic angles using an unmarked straight edge and compass alone. However, in 1980, Hisashi Abe published a method of trisecting any acute angle (*shown opposite centre*) using origami.

Another technique was discovered by Shuzo Fujimoto in 1982. Here you choose a folding sequence which would work if the desired division was already in place, and then proceed with an initial guess, allowing the technique to repeatedly reduce the error. The process can be applied equally well to edge lengths (*below*) and angles (*opposite*). The pattern for one third (0.010101... in binary) is to repeatedly halve the right and then the left segments, RL. For one fifth (0.00110011... in binary), the pattern is RRLL. For one seventh (0.001001... in binary), it is RLL.

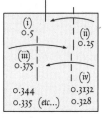

1. First guess at 1/3
2. Half the Right
3. Half the Left
4. Gives a better 1/3, etc...

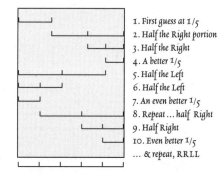

1. First guess at 1/5
2. Half the Right portion
3. Half the Right
4. A better 1/5
5. Half the Left
6. Half the Left
7. An even better 1/5
8. Repeat ... half Right
9. Half Right
10. Even better 1/5
... & repeat, RRLL

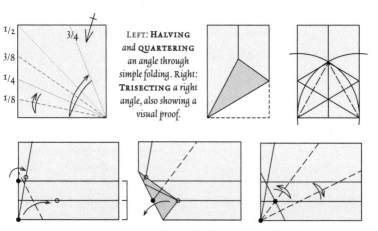

LEFT: **HALVING** and **QUARTERING** an angle through simple folding. Right: **TRISECTING** a right angle, also showing a visual proof.

1/2
3/4
3/8
1/4
1/8

ABOVE: **TRISECTING** an angle, H. Abe (1980). This is a general version of the trisection above.

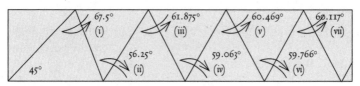

67.5° (i)
61.875° (iii)
60.469° (v)
60.117° (vii)
45°
56.25° (ii)
59.063° (iv)
59.766° (vi)

ABOVE: **FUJIMOTO'S ITERATIVE METHOD** for 60°. At each step, the new angle is bisected. This method exponentially converges to the required angle (here 60°).

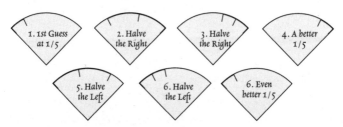

1. 1st Guess at 1/5
2. Halve the Right
3. Halve the Right
4. A better 1/5
5. Halve the Left
6. Halve the Left
6. Even better 1/5

FACING PAGE AND ABOVE: **FUJIMOTO'S ITERATIVE METHOD** for lengths and angles. The pattern for thirds is to halve the remainder, RL, for fifths it is RRLL and for sevenths RLL.

31

SILVER TILINGS
stars and pentagons

Children enjoy making the **EIGHTFOLD STAR** (*1st row below*). Fold the points out of different coloured squares and then glue together.

Silver, or √2, rectangles are closely related to squares and octagons. The diagonal rectangle through a cube is also silver. A silver rectangle can be folded into a near regular **PENTAGON** (*2nd row below*), and they are used in the **ISLAMIC DESIGN** and **PARQUET DEFORMATION** (*opposite*).

The **CAIRO TILE** (*3rd row below*) makes another intriguing tessellation. They are quick to fold by bringing together the opposite corners of a leftover rectangle (*pages 6–7*).

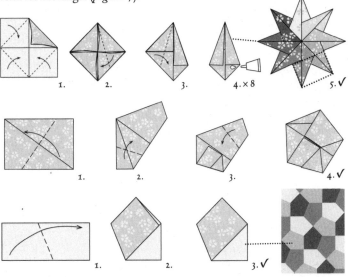

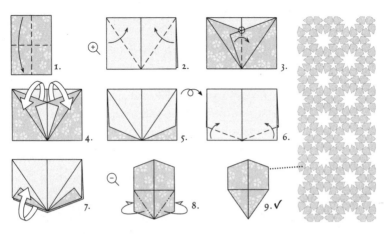

A **Ten-Fold Islamic Design** constructed of tiles folded from silver rectangles.

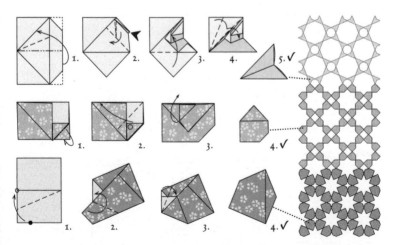

A **Parquet Deformation** from silver rectangles folded into kites, hexagons and pentagons.

PINWHEELS & PURSES
valuable friends

The **MENKO** or **PUZZLE PURSE** is another traditional model. It needs some coordination but gives delightful results. It can remain a pinwheel, or be closed into a purse by interlocking the flaps (*opposite, top*).

This method may be generalised, so similar folds can be used for other pinwheel styles based on hexagons or octagons (*opposite, lower*).

The **REGULAR POLYGONS** required are cut from squares and rectangles. The triangles (*below, a & b*) and hexagons (*c & d*) all use 60° folds (*page 31*). The octagons are derived from squares (*e & f*).

Pleating the corners of an equilateral triangle gives a **HEXAGRAM**. Instead of folding the full length of the mirror lines to find the centre, use pinches to minimise unwanted creases (*right, steps 1–4*).

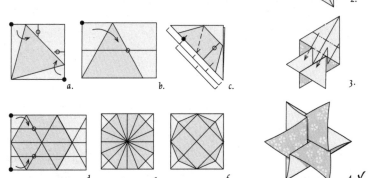

a.   *b.*   *c.*

d.   *e.*   *f.*

1.

2.

3.

4. ✓

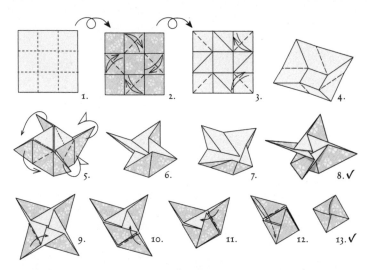

The **MENKO** or **PUZZLE PURSE**, 1. Crease a square into a 3 by 3 grid. 2. Fold one diagonal of each central edge square 3. Crease corner diagonals as indicated. 4. Pinch corners into a 3D box shape. 5-7. Use the second set of diagonals to collapse, rotating flaps anticlockwise. 8. Finished pinwheel. 9-13. To close purse, fold over and interlock flaps, tucking in the last one.

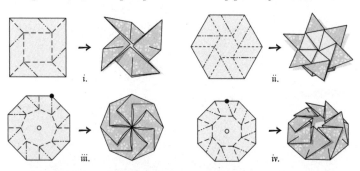

MORE PUZZLE PURSES: Generalising the fold to (i) a square and (ii) a hexagon. For octagons, folding from the vertices (iii) gives a neater purse than folding from the edges (iv).

35

MODULAR STARS
adding up the points

The technique of **MODULAR ORIGAMI** creates shapes by joining together folded units without gluing—instead the parts are slotted or wrapped together to make the finished model (*opposite*).

The **PENTAGRAM** (*below*) uses a modular approach to solve the problem of folding the exact angles of a regular pentagon, improving on the 1:3 approximation from a square. Make the first unit, then slide the second unit onto the first. Fold the small flap on the first unit over the second to lock. Add three more units clockwise to complete.

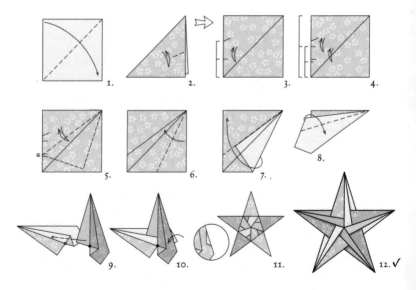

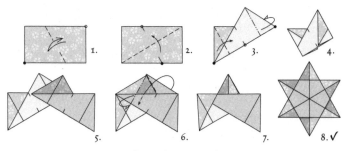

ABOVE: A **SIX-POINTED STAR** *from six bronze rectangles. Bring opposite corners together, pinch edges and join pinch marks to fold the diagonal. Fold through top left corner at right angles to diagonal. Acute corners go to the centre, turn over and repeat. Unfold and wrap units into star.*

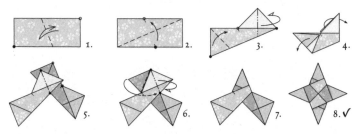

ABOVE: A **FOUR-POINTED STAR** *from four leftover rectangles. Bring opposite corners together, pinch edges and join pinches to fold diagonal. Bisect the corner right angle, then fold the acute corners to the obtuse angled vertex. Turn over and repeat. Unfold and wrap units into the star.*

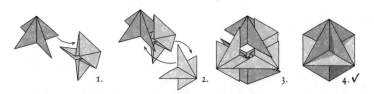

ABOVE: A simple yet effective **SKELETAL OCTAHEDRON**, *made from six Waterbomb Bases (p. 13) slotted together. Use paper clips if the assembly is difficult. Many variations are possible.*

MODULAR POLYHEDRA
folding fabulous facets

The modules used in assembling polyhedra generally form faces or edges, although occasionally they may act as the vertices.

Bronze rectangles have a diagonal that meets the short sides at 60°. The module (*below, step 6*) uses this property to build polyhedra from equilateral triangles. One unit makes a **REGULAR TETRAHEDRON** (*i*) if the mountain and valley folds are swapped over. Three units assemble into a **REGULAR OCTAHEDRON** (*ii*), six a **REGULAR ICOSAHEDRON** (*iii*), twelve a **SNUB CUBE** (*iv*) and thirty a **SNUB DODECAHEDRON** (*v*).

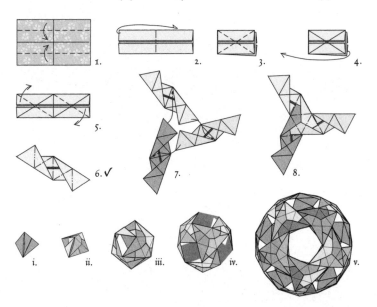

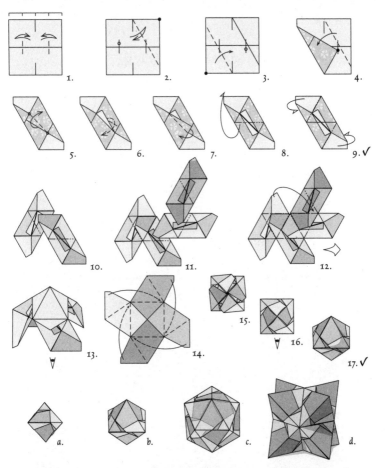

The **Double Equilateral Triangle Unit** starts with a square (steps 1-9). Four units make an **Octahedron** (b, steps 10-17). Mirror image modules are needed to build the **Tetrahedron** (a, two units) and the fragile **Icosahedron** (c, 20 units). The **Stella Octangula** (d) is cunningly constructed from 12 identical units.

Planar Modules
skeletal geometry

All of these origami models occupy space without enclosing any.

A bronze rectangle (*p. 7*) makes a version of the waterbomb base whose triangular flaps are equilateral triangles instead of isosceles right-angled triangles. Fitting twelve together will make a **Skeletal Cuboctahedron** (*below, a*).

Changing the regular hexagons into equilateral triangles makes the **WXYZ** (*opposite top and below, b*). Two bronze rectangles fit inside a square with a small strip of excess paper, which can then be used as flaps to fit into the module pockets.

Six double-square rectangles can be folded into the **XYZ Rhombic** (*opposite lower and below, c*). Left- and right-handed versions are possible.

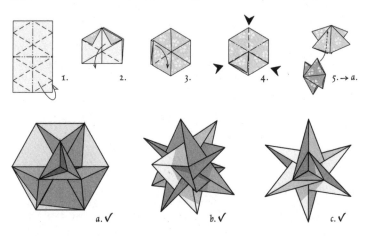

a. ✓   b. ✓   c. ✓

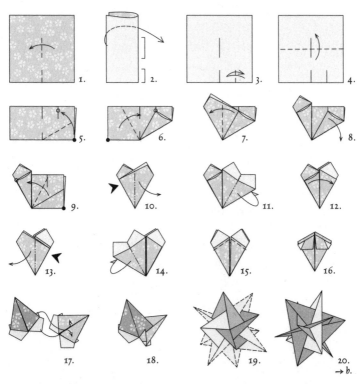

ABOVE (and OPPOSITE-*b*): **WXYZ**. *Use twelve squares of at least 75 mm × 75 mm (3 inches). Four colours are best so that each triangle is different.* BELOW (and OPPOSITE-*c*): The **XYZ RHOMBIC**. *Fold with six 2:1 rectangles. Use three colours to give each rhombus a different tone.*

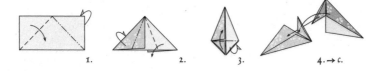

WORKING WITH STRIPS
twisting, folding & weaving

To explore the intriguing properties of a **MÖBIUS STRIP**, take a paper strip, half-twist one end and join together. Cutting the band in half parallel to its edge gives surprising results! Different numbers of half-twists change the outcome, however odd numbers always have one surface and one edge (*right*). Try slicing the bands into thirds and quarters too.

The **TRIHEXAFLEXAGON** is effectively a flattened Möbius Strip of three half-twists. The pinch flex allows you to reveal and hide its faces, hence the name: *tri-* for the three faces and *-hexa-* for the six-sided shape (*opposite top*).

1 half-twist then cut in half

For little fingers, a simpler fold is the kindergarten classic **HEXENTREPPE**—German for *Witch's Staircase*. The loose ends may either be tucked inside or glued (*below*).

2 half-twists (1 full twist) then cut in half

3 half-twists then cut in half

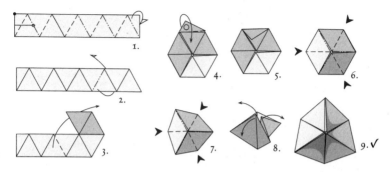

ABOVE: The **TRIHEXAFLEXAGON** 1. Use a strip of paper at least 1:5.77. Precrease a row of equilateral triangles. 2-3. Fold triangles into a hexagon. 4. Glue or tape the last flap to the first. 5. This hexagon has two faces, front and back. 6-8. Pinch flex by squeezing into a 3D shape and opening. 9. This reveals a third face hidden inside. Pinch flex again to show the first face.

RIGHT: Six strips of paper can be woven into a **BALL**. The strips need to be 1:18 or longer. Here, the extra length of a 1 cm by 20 cm strip allows the ends be joined with tape or glue. Alternatively, make a slit at each end to interlock.

BELOW: The **CUBE** weaves six creased strips. 1. Cut eight strips from A4, any six can be used: the key location points arise from 1:2 triangles. 2. Start by weaving one face first, it helps if each end is about the same length. 3. Work the strips for the other faces. Tuck loose ends inside to finish. A few paperclips may aid assembly.

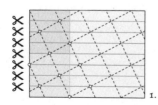

Curves from Straight Lines
spirals, helicoids, hypars and more

A set of straight lines can give the impression of a curve. The four flaps of the **PUZZLE PURSE** (*page 34*) may be repeatedly folded inwards to form a spiral that approximates curves of pursuit (*opposite top*).

For another approximate **SPIRAL**, take a triangle and bisect the angle of the lower left corner. Unfold and make a mountain fold parallel to the base. This fold creates a smaller, similar triangle above the crease which can then be folded in the same way. Continue with this process until all possible folds are made (*below*).

For a three-dimensional curve, take a strip of paper and pleat. Make diagonal folds between the pleats. Pull the ends apart whilst adding a twist to reveal the graceful **HELICOID** (*opposite centre*).

Known to the Bauhaus design school, the **HYPERBOLIC PARABOLOID** uses concentric, alternating pleats to make a sinuous, pliable model. Variations include using a paper disc with circular pleats and a small central disc removed, or the square version as shown (*opposite lower*).

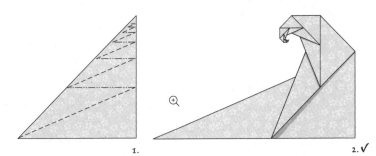

1.   2. ✓

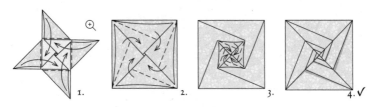

ABOVE: Sequentially interlocking the flaps of a square **PUZZLE PURSE** (p. 34). With repeated folding, the leaves spiral inwards, taking on the approximate form of a four way pursuit curve.

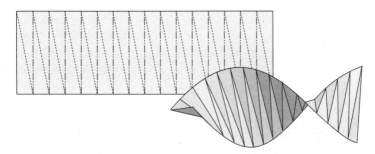

ABOVE: A **HELICOID** can be approximated by dividing a strip into rectangles, all valley folds. Turn over and fold the diagonals of the divisions. The shape can vary from flat to a tight twist.

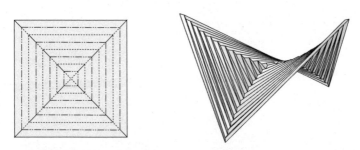

ABOVE: This approximation of a **HYPERBOLIC PARABOLOID** can be made from diagonal folds with concentric square creases of alternating mountain and valley folds.

CORRUGATIONS
waterbombs & chevrons

Origami tessellations require the sharp and accurate precreasing of a single sheet of paper before collapsing into the final form. The results are remarkably organic: it's almost as if they decide their own shape.

For a first attempt at the **WATERBOMB CORRUGATION** (*below*), try a 10 cm square. Note that each row of Xs is shifted horizontally by half a square (*step 6*). On mastering the technique, add more divisions using larger and thicker paper. Work several diagonals at a time, taking care to avoid unnecessary creases. Fold the diagonal of the bottom square, skip a square, then fold the next, and so on.

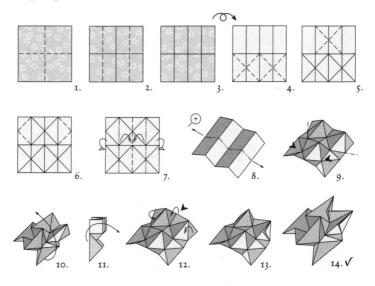

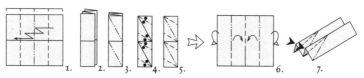

1-17: The **CHEVRON CORRUGATION**: 1. Precrease a square or rectangle into a two-by-two grid. 2. Pleat into quarters. 3. Fold the diagonals of the rectangular sections. 4. Bisect angles. 5. Reinforce creases 6. Open and pleat into quarters. 7. Reverse fold the two peaks. Form the corrugation one row at a time. Note that mountain folds may change into valleys and vice versa.

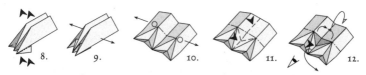

8. Reverse fold the two flaps. 9. Open up. 10. Pull apart so that the central crease is a mountain fold. 11. Push in the centre of the triangle. 12. Continue pushing in the triangle. The shape will be like a right-angled bracket. Note that for greater clarity, not all creases are shown here.

13. Fold side flaps down whilst pushing in front faces. 14. Open up a little. 15. Make valley folds in the M shape, then use creases to make two reverse folds. 16. Mountain fold the two corners. Reverse fold central peak. 17. Valley fold the two corners. Reverse fold the central flap to complete.

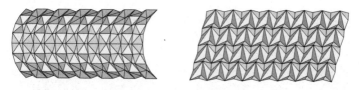

ABOVE: **EXTENDED TESSELLATIONS**. Waterbomb (LEFT) and Chevron (RIGHT) corrugations can be applied to larger grids. The resulting flexible sheets can be shaped into many curious forms.

DEFORMABLE SURFACES
remarkable metamaterials

Origami's ability to transform flat sheets into a myriad of forms can be employed in many practical applications.

Folded **CUPS** and **BOXES** (*p. 11*) have been around for centuries, with novel containers still being invented. Origami has inspired the safe folding of **AIR BAGS** in cars, the design of collapsible **KAYAKS**, and has even been applied to the complexity of **PROTEIN FOLDING**.

An intriguing use of the waterbomb corrugation (*p. 46*) creates **MEDICAL STENTS**. Made from a nickel/titanium alloy, the stents are inserted into the body to keep open veins and arteries (*opposite top*).

Folding is an ideal way to store large structures in a small volume. A number of origami-based designs exist for **SHELTERS** where their ease of transportation and construction makes them perfect for extreme situations, such as emergencies or polar and space exploration (*below*).

Another useful mechanism is the **MIURA-ORI MAP FOLD**. Its compact folded state can be expanded in one motion by pulling opposite ends, or when open, it can be rapidly closed by pushing the ends together (*opposite mid*).

The map fold is one of several designs proposed for satellite **SOLAR PANELS**. These combine the advantages of using minimal storage space for launch with a relatively simple deployment procedure on reaching orbit (*opposite lower*).

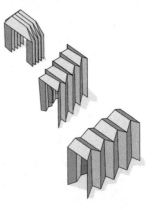

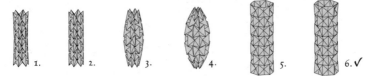

ABOVE: A **WATERBOMB CORRUGATION MEDICAL STENT**. The small initial diameter allows the stent to be easily inserted, then quickly expanded to support collapsed arteries and veins.

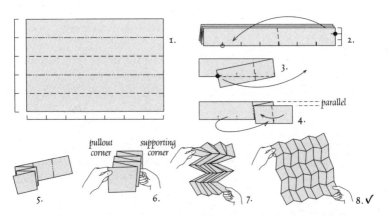

ABOVE: The **MIURA-ORI MAP FOLD**: Precrease, dividing long edge into sevenths and pleating the short into fifths. Fold the point one third down the right edge across to a point one seventh along the bottom. Make a series of parallel pleats, repeating the same angles in each "Z" fold.

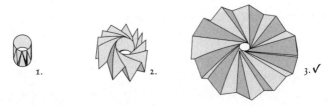

ABOVE: A biaxial folding **DEPLOYABLE STRUCTURE** design for satellite solar panels.

CURVES
petals & flowers

Most origami uses straight lines. However, curves appear in origami in a number of ways: from the starting shape, forming cones by folding at a point, making tubes or using curved lines as folds.

The **LOTUS** (*opposite top*) is best folded from a square of stiff cloth or a fabric-like paper, such as *washi* or napkins—ordinary paper may tear when peeling the petals. If the square is small, or too thick, then try folding twice to the centre instead of three times.

The **LAZY SUSAN** is another traditional design that can be used as a serving dish for finger foods (*opposite lower*). Its shape echoes that of old Chinese coins, which could be strung together through a central hole.

Circles are the most simple curved starting shape. Some argue that circles folded with straight lines renders the curves irrelevant or inconvenient. However, circles make certain angles easier to fold than rectangles, and curved edges allow models to rock or roll.

Inspired by the elegant lattice structures of R. Buckminster Fuller [1895–1983], the **SPHERICAL SKELETAL ICOSIDODECAHEDRON** (*right*) is folded from circles, allowing the 72° angles to be made without tools. When six 'bow tie' modules have been made, glue the folded edges together to complete the model.

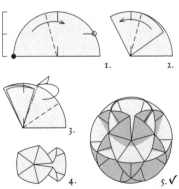

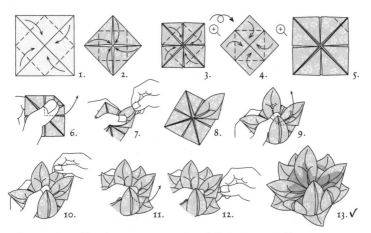

The **Lotus**. 1. Fold corners to centre once 2. twice 3. thrice, turn over. 4. Fold corners to centre. 5. To make petals, fold a tip in. 6. Hold tip, peel flap from behind. 7. Lift flap and curve. 8. Completed petals. Repeat for other corners. 9-10. Fold second petals. 11-13. Fold final petals.

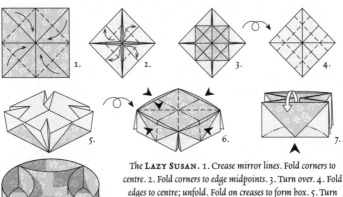

The **Lazy Susan**. 1. Crease mirror lines. Fold corners to centre. 2. Fold corners to edge midpoints. 3. Turn over. 4. Fold edges to centre; unfold. Fold on creases to form box. 5. Turn over. 6. Push in centre and squeeze corners to collapse into an X, then collapse flat. 7. Slide finger into a pocket to open. Simultaneously, curve base. 8. Repeat for each pocket.

51

CURVED FOLDS & CRUMPLING
off the straight & narrow

Consistent **CURVED FOLDS** are harder to make than straight ones. Practice by folding circular arcs on a sheet of paper (*below*). The easiest way is to score first with a ballpoint pen that has run out of ink. Find a circular object to score around, like a bowl or tin. Then alternate folding the mountain and valley creases by turning the paper over. Experiment by varying the gaps between the arcs and where the centres lie.

David Huffman [1925–1999], creator of Huffman coding, was one of several pioneers of curved folds. The elegant curves of his **HEXAGONAL TOWER** are circular arcs, whilst the **ARCHES** are parabolic (*opposite top and middle*). The arches are related to the Waterbomb Corrugation.

It is no coincidence that arcs from circles, ellipses and parabolas are used for curved folds. Huffman treated ruling lines as 'light rays' travelling across the paper. Curved folds 'refract' the rays, changing their paths and thus the direction of curvature of the paper (*opposite middle*). The curves that transform rays from one point source to another are conic sections.

As an alternative, **CRUMPLING** the paper creates countless tiny creases. This has been a source of innovation for many organic and abstract subjects (*opposite lower*).

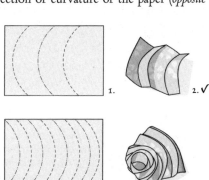

52

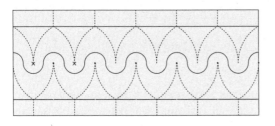 

ABOVE: **HUFFMAN'S HEXAGONAL TOWER WITH CUSPS**. *The wavy line is drawn with semicircles of unit radius. The cusps are ⅙ circular arcs of four units radius, centred on the ×.*

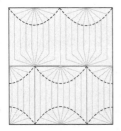  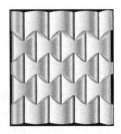

ABOVE: **HUFFMAN'S ARCHES**. *Each full "brick" is a 5:6 rectangle. The additional grey lines on the crease pattern show the 'light rays' being refracted by the parabolic 'lenses'. One way to make the curves consistent is to use a cardboard template. Draw around the template with an inkless ballpoint pen. Score the creases then gently shape. It is hard, but feasible for experienced folders.*

LEFT: **A CRUMPLED MUSHROOM**. *Use strong, thin 20-40 gsm tissue, tracing or butcher's paper—even a single ply of a napkin will work. Squeeze the paper in one direction without twisting. Open out and invert. Repeat several times until the sheet is elastic, Squash, flatten and fold into the desired shape. The final working area is small compared with the starting size.*

PAPER CUTS
slash & grab

Cutting adds many degrees of freedom to paper engineering. All the cuts on these pages start from a raw or folded edge and so can be easily made with scissors instead of a knife.

For youngsters, the traditional **MONKEY CLIMBING THE MOUNTAIN** creates an unusual action model (*opposite, top*). The cut off corner–the 'monkey'–will, with a little practice, climb up the centre folds and pop out of the peak. For fun, draw a monkey face on the moving piece.

In Scandinavia, Christmas trees are decorated with **JULEKURVER**, woven baskets filled with sweet treats. Danish author Hans Christian Andersen [1805–75] was a keen paper-cutter and is known to have made them. They may have more or fewer divisions, and larger versions can make delightful paper bonnets (*opposite, lower*).

The intriguing **POPUP SPINNER** (*below*) is from a student at Musahino Art University. Paper is fine for a small model, but card is more stable.

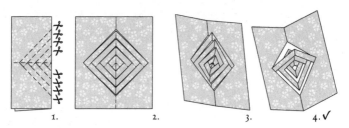

A **POPUP SPINNER**. 1. *Fold in half. Cut the double layer at the fold, stopping the upper cuts exactly at halfway, but leaving the lower cuts a little short of this line.* 2. *Open up.* 3. *Start with the outermost square: make valley and mountain folds, rotating sections whilst working towards centre.* 4. *The vertical folds are mountains above the central guideline and valleys below.*

54

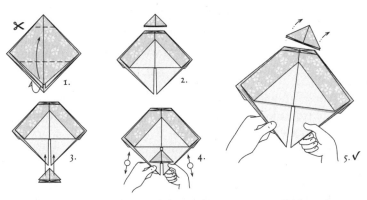

MONKEY CLIMBING THE MOUNTAIN 1. Start with a preliminary fold (page 12).
2. Cut off top. 3. Open a little and slide the top -the 'monkey' -onto base by overlapping. 4. Hold
and wiggle to make the monkey climb up inside. 5. Experiment by adjusting grip and wiggle speed.

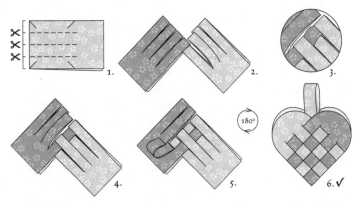

The **JULEKURVER** is made from two 1:3 rectangles. 1. Fold sheets in half, short edges together.
Divide folded edge into quarters and cut. 2. Place at right angles, slip right finger into left. 3.
Slip left finger into right. 4. Alternate inside and outside until fully woven. 5. Move up, weave in
second fingers the opposite way round. 6. Continue weaving until finished then trim the open ends
of the basket into a heart shape. Glue on a strip of paper to make the handle.

KIRIGAMI
the cutting edge

It has been known for a long time that an approximate **PENTAGON** can be made from a folded square with one cut, whilst a different cut gives a **PENTAGRAM** (*below*). A straight cut to a piece of folded paper can make a single polygon, multiple disjoint polygons, nested polygons, adjoining polygons, or even line segments and points.

Kirigami 切り紙 means 'cut paper' in Japanese and involves cutting and discarding paper, whilst *kirikomi* 切り込み – 'notch'– uses slits to simplify folding. The **UNICORN** (*opposite top*) needs three cuts to create the seven flaps for the legs, tail, head and horn. Avoiding the cuts would complicate folding and make the structure less efficient: paper would have to be hidden inside and the result would be smaller and thicker.

Although rare, some traditional origami does use cuts. The **KABUTO** helmet, for instance, transforms into the **GOLDFISH** (*lower opposite*). Of course, the big disadvantage of cutting is that it is irreversible, so it is wise to follow the carpenter's adage to "measure twice, cut once".

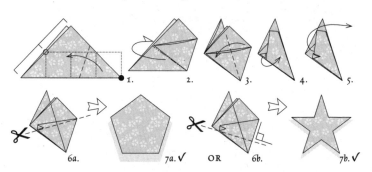

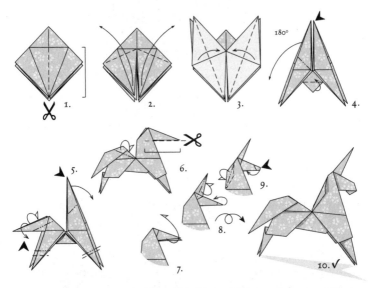

This mystical **UNICORN** is based on the traditional Somersaulting Horse design. Start with step 5 of the Flapping Bird (page. 19), being sure to make the cuts carefully and precisely.

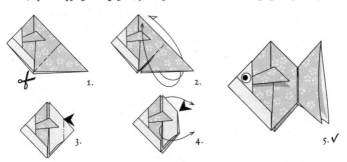

The **GOLDFISH**. Start with step 6 of the Kabuto (page 9), open and squash the back. Cut nearly halfway through both layers. Outside reverse fold, inside reverse fold and pull to unwrap tail.

WIIY FOLD?
the perception of origami

Folding mechanisms are found all across nature—from insects and birds tucking away their wings, to plant leaves unfurling, and the crumpling, buckling and wrinkling of rock, magma and skin.

Origami has many practical applications. However, it is also enjoyable for its own sake: it is craft, art, game, puzzle, relaxation and more. The sheet is almost magically transformed into a result that can easily be unfolded back to its starting point.

For some paperfolders, the square symbolises a belief in the universe and the Buddha-nature in all things. Origami author Eric Kenneway [1930-1985] observed that *Zen*, the Japanese way of developing self-awareness, is characterised by preferring simplicity over complexity.

Some believe that rather than only expressing "empty aestheticism", the practice of origami should reveal a holistic attitude to life and nature. Just as contemplation may lead to enlightenment, so folding paper in the right way might also lead to an awakening of hearts and minds.

COVER: *adapted from an engraving in "La Nature" by Emile and Auguste Tilly, designed by Charles Gilbert-Martin, 1885.*
HALF-TITLE PAGE: *"A Magician Turns Sheets of Paper Into Birds" by Katsushika Hokusai, 1819.*
TITLE PAGE: *from "Hiden Senbazuru Orikata" by Akisato Ritō, illustrated by Takehara Shunsensai, 1797.*
THIS PAGE: *from "Ehon Seiro Bijin Awase" by Suzuki Harunobu, 1770.*